Volume 2

CW00539147

CLARINET SOLOS
with piano accompaniment
Arranged and edited by Thea King

INDEX

Chester Music

(A Division of Music Sales Limited)
8/9 Frith Street, London W1V 5TZ
Exclusive distributors: Music Sales Limited, Newmarket Road,
Bury St. Edmunds, Suffolk IP33 3YB.

8-95

1

Andante from Concerto for Clarinet and Military Band

RIMSKY-KORSAKOV

2
Menuetto from Quartet in C minor, Op. 4

CRUSELL

TRIO

D.C. Menuetto al fine

D.C. Menuetto al fine

3
Andante from Konzertstück in D minor, Op. 114

MENDELSSOHN

4
Allegro from Wind Sextet, Op. 71

BEETHOVEN

5
Allegretto from Introduction, Theme and Variations

WEBER

16

1

Andante from Concerto for Clarinet and Military Band

RIMSKY-KORSAKOV

2
Menuetto from Quartet in C minor, Op. 4

CRUSELL

Fine

TRIO

D.C. Menuetto al fine

3

Andante from Konzertstück in D minor, Op. 114

MENDELSSOHN

4

Allegro from Wind Sextet, Op. 71

BEETHOVEN

5

Allegretto from Introduction, Theme and Variations

WEBER

6

Andante moderato from Concerto in B♭, Op. 11

CRUSELL

7
Moderato, first movement from Concerto No. 4 in D

MOLTER

8

Allegretto from "The Seasons"

GLAZOUNOV

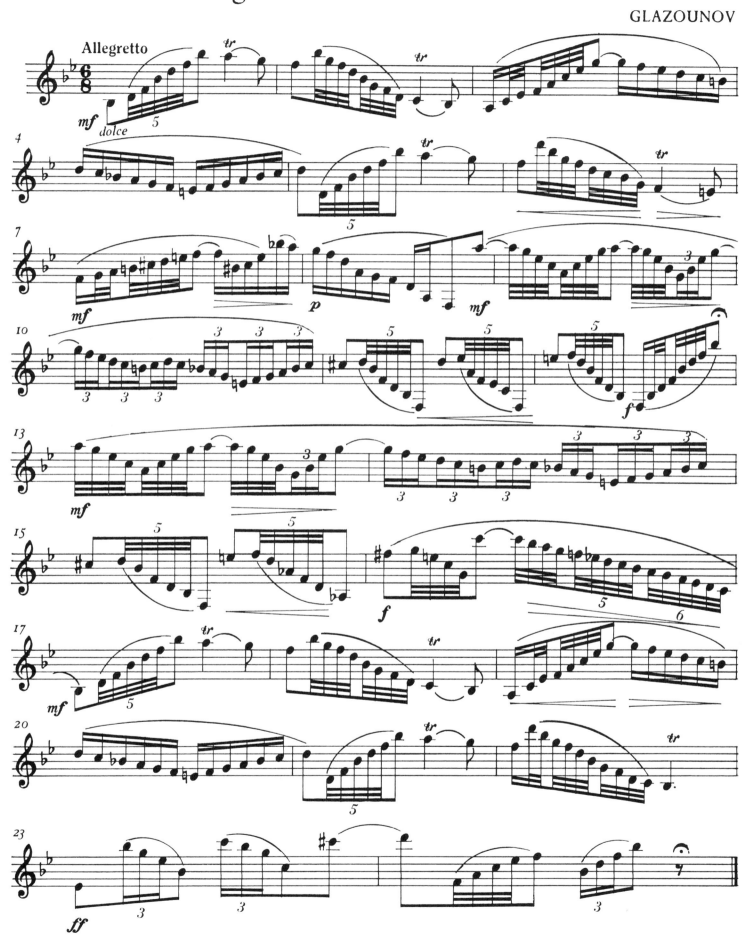

5/01 (40346)

Printed by Halstan & Co. Ltd., Amersham, Bucks., England

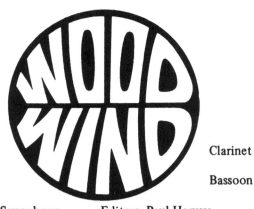

Flute   Editor: Trevor Wye   Clarinet   Editor: Thea King

Oboe   Editor: James Brown   Bassoon   Editor: William Waterhouse

Saxophone   Editor: Paul Harvey

A growing collection of volumes from Chester Music, containing a
wide range of pieces from different periods.

CLARINET SOLOS VOLUME I		CLARINET SOLOS VOLUME II	
Bizet	Entr'acte from Carmen	Beethoven	Allegro (Finale) from Wind Sextet Op. 71
Labor	Allegretto from Quintet for Clarinet, Strings and Piano	Crusell	Minuet from Quartet in C minor Op. 4
Lefèvre	Allegro from Sonata No. 3	Crusell	Andante Moderato from Concerto in B♭ Op. 11
Mozart	Minuet from Serenade for Wind Octet K. 375	Glazounov	Allegretto from the ballet The Seasons
Mozart	Il Mio Tesoro	Mendelssohn	Andante from Konzertstück in D minor Op. 114
Schubert	Trio from the Minuet of Octet, Op. 166	Molter	Moderato from Concerto in D
Schubert	Allegretto from Symphony No. 3	Rimsky-Korsakov	Andante from Concerto for Clarinet and Military Band
Tchaikovsky	Allegro Con Grazia from Symphony No. 6	Weber	From Introduction, Theme and Variations

Also available:
CLARINET DUETS VOLUMES I, II & III
Further details on request

Chester Music

(A Division of Music Sales Limited)
8/9 Frith Street, London W1V 5TZ
Exclusive distributors: Music Sales Limited, Newmarket Road,
Bury St. Edmunds, Suffolk IP33 3YB.

6

Andante moderato from Concerto in B♭, Op. 11

CRUSELL

7

Moderato, first movement from Concerto No. 4 in D

MOLTER

26

8
Allegretto from "The Seasons"

GLAZOUNOV

5/01 (40346)

Printed by Halstan & Co. Ltd., Amersham, Bucks., England

NOTES

1. Andante from Concerto for Clarinet and Military Band
    Nikolai Rimsky-Korsakov (1844 - 1908)

    The concerto is accompanied by military band, and is quite a short work, in three
    linked movements.

2. Menuetto from Quartet in C minor, Op. 4
    Bernhardt Crusell (1775 - 1838)

    This little-known Finnish composer lived most of his life in Sweden, equally talented
    as a clarinettist, composer and translator of operas. There are two more works for
    this combination of clarinet and string trio.

3. Andante from Konzertstück in D minor Op. 114
    Felix Mendelssohn-Bartholdy (1809 - 1847)

    There are two 'concert pieces', Op. 113 and 114 for clarinet, basset-horn and piano,
    written for Heinrich Baermann and his son Carl, who doubtless performed them with
    the composer. This movement is mainly a duet for the two wind instruments and in
    this arrangement I have not altered the clarinet part in any way.

4. Allegro (Finale) from Wind Sextet Op. 71
    Ludwig van Beethoven (1770 - 1827)

    Wind bands were maintained by many courts in the eighteenth century, and must
    have helped many composers to earn their keep. This march is scored for clarinets,
    bassoons and horns, and there is also a more well-known Octet Op. 103, which
    includes oboes.

5. Allegretto from Introduction, Theme and Variations
    Carl Maria von Weber (1786 - 1826)

    This is perhaps the least known of the many excellent solo pieces for clarinet which
    Weber so generously provided, and is accompanied by string quartet. I have selected
    the theme and three variations.

6. Andante Moderato from Concerto in Bb Op. 11
    Bernhardt Crusell (1775 - 1838)

    The song-like quality of this piece reminds one of Mozart's clarinet writing, and fore-
    shadows Crusell's interest in opera and his many compositions for voice. The last
    section of the movement has been simplified.

7. Moderato, first movement from Concerto in D
    Johann Melchior Molter (1695 - 1765)

    Molter worked as Kapellmeister to the Margrave Karl Wilhelm of Baden-Durlach at
    Karlsruhe, and wrote four concertos for the high D clarinet, now thought to be the
    earliest solo works for our instrument. The chances to play them on the D clarinet
    are rare, and need much embrouchure stamina, so I have transposed the part down a
    fourth and shortened the tuttis, in order to give a taste of this very interesting early
    style of writing.

8. Allegretto from the ballet *The Seasons*
    Alexander Glazounov (1865 - 1936)

    Glazounov delighted in orchestral colouring, and this little number in the ballet
    spotlights the clarinet charmingly. It needs elegance, rather than speed, to make its
    effect.